عاشت مين مين مع ابنها الصغير شن لي. وكان بيتهم قريباً من النهر.
واجتهدت مين مين في عملها كثيراً حتى توفر العيش لنفسها وابنها.
كان لها حقل أرز صغير وبعض الدجاجات ومزرعة صغيرة
للخضروات وقليل من السمك النهري وجاموسة عجوز.

Mei Mei lived with her young son, Chun Li. Their home was close to the
river. Mei Mei worked hard to make a living for them both. She had a
small paddyfield, some chickens, a small plot of vegetables, some fresh
water fish and an old buffalo.

دموع التنين
The Dragon's Tears

Story by Manju Gregory
Pictures by Guo Le

Arabic by Dr Sajida Fawzi

كانت البحيرات الأربع والعشرين عند منحنى نهر مين من أجمل ما يكون
يعمها الهدوء والسلام. وجلست مين مين على ضفة النهر تتذكر.
تذكرت الوقت الذي لم يكن هناك أي بحيرات.
تذكرت أوقاتا صعبة و حزينة.

In the curve of the river Min the lakes looked calm and peaceful.
They were filled with beauty. Twenty four in all.
Mei Mei sat by the banks of the river remembering.
She remembered a time when there were no lakes at all.
She remembered a time of struggle and sadness.

كان شن لي يصطاد السمك يوميا من النهر. وفي احد الأيام و عندما سحب خيط السنارة وجده أصعب من المعتاد وظن أنه سيكون صيدا كبيرا. وإذا بموجة عظيمة من الماء يتناثر منها رذاذا فضي وتقفز منها سمكة ذهبية.

Chun Li fished daily down by the river. One day the pull of the line was much, much more than usual. This promised to be a fine catch, he thought. With a mighty splash and a silvery spray a golden fish flipped out of the water.

وقالت

...and spoke...

"أعدني إلى الماء من فضلك يا شن لي وسوف أكافئك مكافأة حسنة."

وشهق شن لي قائلا "إنها سمكة تتكلم!"

وعندما كان يسحب السنارة من فمها بعناية فاذا بلؤلؤة براقة كبيرة تنزلق رويدا رويدا إلى يده، ولم يكن قد رأى لؤلؤة جميلة مثلها أبدا. وقالت السمكة وهي في طريقها تختفي في الماء "ستجعلك هذه اللؤلؤة السحرية غنياً."

"Chun Li, will you please throw me back in the water? I will repay you well."
Chun Li gasped: "A talking fish!" He carefully removed the hook from the fish's mouth and as he did so, a huge and gleaming pearl rolled gently onto his hand. He had never seen such a beautiful gem.
"This magic pearl will make your fortune," said the fish as it disappeared into the water.

أسرع شن لي عائدا إلى البيت مناديا أمه. وتعجبت أمه عندما رأت تلك اللؤلؤة الرائعة، وأخبرها شن لي بأنها لؤلؤة سحرية. وضع شن لي اللؤلؤة بعناية فوق كيس من الأرز. وفجأة أصبح الكيس كيسين!

Chun Li ran back home, calling out to his mother. She was astonished to see such a magnificent pearl. Chun Li told her it was a magic pearl. He placed it carefully on top of a sack of rice.
Straight away there were two rice sacks!

ثم وضعوا اللؤلؤة بين حزمة من الجزر، وإذا بها تصبح حزمتين من الجزر! وجعلت من إناء الفلفل إناءين من الفلفل.

Next they placed the magic pearl amongst a bunch of carrots.
Two bunches of carrots!
A bowl of chillies. Two bowls of chillies!

ومن صينية من فاكهة اللاشين،
صينيتين من فاكهة اللاشين!

A tray of prickly lychees.
Two trays of prickly lychees!

ومن عنقود موز ناضج،
عنقودين ناضجين!

A bunch of ripe bananas. Two
bunches of ripe bananas!

ومن سلة بيض طازج،
سلتين من البيض الطازج!

A basket of newly laid eggs.
Two baskets of newly laid eggs!

وأنعم الاله على الولد و أمه بنعمة عظيمة.

The boy and his mother were blessed with great good fortune.

واستعملوا ثروتهم استعمالا حكيماً. أشركوا اُلآخرين معهم وأحبوا العطاء.
وفرح بعض الناس لفرحهم وشك بعضهم في الأمر. و شعر قسم منهم
بالحسد بينما قرر اُلآخرون زيارتهم!

They used their fortune wisely. They shared well and enjoyed giving.
Some people felt happy for them. Some people felt suspicious. Others
were filled with envy and a few decided to pay them a visit!

كانت مين مين مشغولة بإطعام الدجاج عندما سمعت صوت خيول مهرولة تقترب وتقترب
وبعد وقت قصير وجدت نفسها محاطة بجماعة من الناس القساة الغاضبين.
وسألوها كيف أصبحت بهذا الثراء العظيم.
وارتعبت مين مين ومن شدة خوفها أخبرتهم القصة كاملة.
أراد الناس أن يعرفوا شيئا واحداً فقط.
"أين اللؤلؤة السحرية؟"

One day, as usual, Mei Mei was busy feeding her chickens. She heard the sound of
galloping horses coming nearer and nearer and very soon she was surrounded by a
mean and angry crowd.
They demanded to know how she had become so prosperous.
Mei Mei was terrified and in her terror she told the whole story.
Now the crowd only wanted to know one thing. "Where is the magic pearl?"

ولم تجب مين مين، فأزاحوها عن الطريق ودخلوا بيتها الصغير.

Mei Mei did not answer.
They pushed her out of the way and entered her little house.

نثروا وقلبوا كل شيء وقعت عليه أعينهم.

وفتح أحدهم باب الدولاب الذي كان شن لي مختبئاً فيه.

ومن شدة خوفه وضع شن لو اللؤلؤة السحرية في فمه.

وسحبه الناس من الدولاب وهم يصرخون "أفرغ جيوبك! إرفع يديك!"

وصرخ أحدهم "إفتح فمك!"

وفتح شن لي فمه بطيئاً ولكن اللؤلؤة لم تكن فيه، كان قد ابتلعها!

وكف الناس الغاضبون عن التفتيش وانصرفوا.

They upturned everything in sight. Then someone opened the door of the
cupboard where Chun Li was hiding. In his fright he quickly put the magic pearl
into his mouth.
The people dragged him out and screamed, "Empty your pockets!
Hold out your hands!"
"Open your mouth!" shouted someone.
Chun Li slowly opened his mouth. But there was no pearl. He had swallowed it!
The angry crowd gave up their search and rode away.

هدأت مين مين إبنها الذي كان يرتعش فقد اصابته الحمى واصبح جسمه ساخناً.
وصرخ طالباً قليلا من الماء ليقلل من حرارة جسمه. في البداية جلبت له مين مين
أقداحاً من الماء وبعد ذلك صبت عليه سطولاً من الماء ولكنه لم يستطع أن يروي
عطشه. وأخذته إلى النهر حيث شرب ماءً أكثر وأكثر. ولكن شن لي ازداد سخونة
وشعر وكأن جسمه ملتهب.

Mei Mei comforted her son who was shaking. His body was hot and feverish. He cried for
some water to cool him down. First Mei Mei brought him cups of water, next she poured
pails of water but he could not quench his thirst. She took him to the river where he drank
even more water. But Chun Li just became hotter. His body felt as though it was on fire.

وتصاعد البخار من فمه واندلعت النار من أنفه ولاحظت مين مين أن جسم الولد
قد بدأ يتغير. فاصبح له حراشف كبيرة لامعة وذنب طويل مضيىً. فقد تحول تنّين.
شن لي إلى

والأكثر من هذا أخذ شن لي يرتفع و يرتفع إلى السماء الزرقاء.
وبكت مين مين على ابنها الغالي وهو يبتعد و يبتعد حيث يكاد يختفي عن الأنظار.

Steam poured from his mouth, fire flared from his nostrils and Mei
Mei saw that the boy's body was changing. Chun Li had changed into
a dragon.
What's more, he was rising, up up into the bright blue sky.
Mei Mei wept for her precious son as he moved further away into the
clouds, almost out of sight.

وتوسلت إليه أمه ليعود. وأدار شن لي رأسه بطيئاً وسقطت دمعة غزيرة كبيرة من عينيه الكبيرتين الحزينتين. وسقطت الدمعة في منحنى نهر مين وإذا ببحيرة لؤلؤية جميلة تظهر في مكانها. وسقطت دمعة أخرى وأخرى وأخرى وكل دمعة تحولت إلى بحيرة حتى كان هناك ٢٤ بحيرة.

She begged for him to come back. Chun Li's head turned slowly and from the huge sad eyes fell a great wet tear. It dropped in a curve of the river Min and a beautiful pearly lake was born. There fell another tear and another and another. Each turned into a lake until there were twenty four in all.

ولم تستطع مين مين أن تنظر إلى أعلى ولكنها عندما نظرت إلى أعلى لم
تصدق َعينيها. فإذا بإبنها الصغير شن لي يظهر من خلال الضباب فوق
البحيرة مسرعاً نحوها فمدت ذراعيها -ستقباله.
وأضاءت البحيرات ببريقها الأرض الخصبة حولها.

Mei Mei could barely look up. When she did a most magical thing
happened. Her young boy, Chun Li, was rising from the mists across the
lake and running towards her. She reached out her arms to receive him.

The lakes glistened in the fertile landscape.